$100M Offers
Made Easy

Create Your Own Irresistible Offers by
Turning ChatGPT into Alex Hormozi

Benjamin Preston

Contents

FREE Bonus

As a Token of Appreciation for Your Support

I 'd like to express my heartfelt gratitude for choosing to explore the world of irresistible offers with "**100M Offers Made Easy**." Your passion for business growth is commendable and I'm excited to have you on this journey.

As a special thank you, I have a gift for you.

Author Insights, showing you how to turn your favorite author into your personal business coach, with the magic of ChatGPT.

AUTHOR INSIGHTS

Turn your favorite author into your personal Business coach with ChatGPT

Scan the QR Code below to get your Free copy of **Author Insights**

BENJAMIN PRESTON

Introduction

Welcome to the world of irresistible offers, where the art of ChatGPT meets the mind of Alex Hormozi. If you're a fan of Alex Hormozi, you know that he's a force to be reckoned with in the world of entrepreneurship. His insights, strategies, and unrelenting drive have helped countless entrepreneurs transform their businesses and lives. Now, imagine if you could tap into that same depth of knowledge and skill to supercharge your own entrepreneurial journey.

In this book, we're going to take you on a transformative journey, showing you how to harness the incredible capabilities of ChatGPT and infuse them with the unique depth and style that define Alex Hormozi's work. Whether you're a seasoned business owner looking to scale to new heights or just starting your entrepreneurial adventure, the principles and strategies within these pages will empower you to craft irresistible offers that can propel your business to the coveted $100 million dollar mark.

The Power of Turning ChatGPT into Alex Hormozi

You might be wondering, "What does ChatGPT have to do with Alex Hormozi?" At first glance, it might seem like an unlikely pairing. ChatGPT is an artificial intelligence language model, while Alex Hormozi is a real-world entrepreneur and business strategist. However, the magic lies in the fusion of these two worlds, and the power that emerges from their synergy.

Imagine having a virtual Alex Hormozi at your side, to help you brainstorm, refine, and execute your business ideas with precision and insight. That's exactly what you'll achieve as you progress through this book. We'll guide you step by step, revealing how you can leverage ChatGPT's vast knowledge and linguistic abilities to emulate the strategies, depth, and skills that have made Alex Hormozi's offers so irresistible.

But before we dive deeper into the practical aspects of crafting your own $100 million dollar offer, let's take a moment to understand the significance of irresistible offers and why they're the cornerstone of Alex Hormozi's success.

The Essence of Irresistible Offers

An irresistible offer is more than just a sales pitch or a marketing gimmick. It's a carefully crafted proposition that captivates your audience, solves their deepest problems, and compels them to take action. Think about the last time you made a purchase that you couldn't let pass you by, even though you hadn't planned on buying anything that day. That's the power of an irresistible offer at work.

Alex Hormozi has made a name for himself by consistently creating offers that people can't say no to. Whether it's a fitness program, a coaching service, or a business growth strategy, his offers have a magnetic quality that draws people in and keeps them coming back for more.

So, what sets an irresistible offer apart from the rest? It's a combination of several key elements:

- **Value:** An irresistible offer provides immense value to the customer. It addresses their pain points, fulfills their desires, and offers a clear solution to their problems.

- **Clarity:** The offer is presented in a clear and straightforward manner. There's no confusion or ambiguity about what the customer will receive and how it will benefit them.

- **Uniqueness:** It stands out in a crowded marketplace. An irresistible offer has a unique selling proposition that makes it different from the competition.

- **Emotion:** It taps into the customer's emotions, creating a strong desire to take action. People buy based on emotion and justify their purchase with logic.

- **Scarcity and Urgency:** There's a sense of scarcity or urgency associated with the offer, encouraging the customer to act quickly to avoid missing out.

- **Risk Reversal:** The offer minimizes or eliminates the customer's perceived risk. This could include money-back guarantees or trial periods.

- **Compelling Storytelling:** It's presented in a way that resonates with the customer's story and journey, making them
  feel understood and connected.

Alex Hormozi has mastered the art of combining these elements to create offers that not only drive sales but also build long-term customer loyalty. And now, you're about to learn how to do the same with the help of ChatGPT.

Turning ChatGPT into Your Irresistible Offer Crafting Partner

Imagine having Alex Hormozi himself sitting across from you, guiding you through the process of creating your own irresistible offers. While that might remain a dream for many, we're here to tell you that you can achieve something remarkably close to it by turning ChatGPT into your virtual offer crafting partner.

ChatGPT, powered by OpenAI's cutting-edge artificial intelligence, has been trained on a vast corpus of text from the internet, including countless articles, books, and websites. It's a treasure trove of knowledge and linguistic prowess, ready to assist you in your entrepreneurial endeavors. But it's not just about having access to information; it's about how you use that information to your advantage.

In the pages that follow, we'll show you how to harness ChatGPT's capabilities and channel the spirit of Alex Hormozi into your offer creation process. You'll learn how to:

- **Leverage ChatGPT's Knowledge:** Discover the art of asking ChatGPT the right questions to extract valuable insights and information that can supercharge your offer.

- **Infuse Alex Hormozi's Style:** Understand the nuances of Alex Hormozi's writing and speaking style, and use ChatGPT to emulate it in your offer copy.

- **Craft Irresistible Offers:** Follow a step-by-step process to create offers that are not only compelling but also authentic to your brand and audience.

- **Test and Optimize:** Learn how to continually test and refine your offers, just as Alex Hormozi does, to ensure they remain irresistible and relevant.

By the time you finish reading this book, you'll have the tools, knowledge, and confidence to craft offers that have the potential to transform your business and your life.

Chapter One

The Psychology of Irresistible Offers

In the world of entrepreneurship, the concept of irresistible offers reigns supreme. It's the secret sauce that turns casual browsers into enthusiastic buyers and transforms businesses from mediocre to magnificent. But what exactly is the psychology behind these irresistible offers, and how can you harness their power for your own entrepreneurial journey?

The Mindset of the Customer

To craft offers that your audience simply can't resist, you need to delve into the mindset of the customer. Understanding why people make purchasing decisions is the first step toward creating offers that align with their desires and motivations.

1. Emotional Connection: Irresistible offers establish a deep emotional connection with potential buyers. We'll explore how to create marketing messages that resonate with your audience's emotions, making them more likely to take action.

2. Trust and Credibility: Building trust is paramount. We'll delve into strategies for establishing your credibility and trustworthiness, ensuring that your offers are seen as authentic and reliable.

3. Fears and Aspirations: Every customer has fears and aspirations. Irresistible offers address these by alleviating fears and helping customers achieve their aspirations. We'll uncover how to identify and cater to these fundamental human needs.

Crafting Offers That Stand Out

Irresistible offers are not haphazardly thrown together; they are carefully crafted with specific elements that make them stand out. In this section, we'll dissect these crucial components, exploring how each contributes to the overall allure of an offer.

1. Crafting Unique Value: We'll dive deep into the concept of value and how to create a value proposition that speaks directly to your target audience. You'll learn how to identify your unique selling points and communicate them effectively.

2. The Power of Storytelling: Irresistible offers often rely on storytelling to captivate the audience. We'll discuss the importance of storytelling in your marketing and offer creation and provide practical tips on crafting compelling narratives.

3. Scarcity, Urgency, and Exclusivity: Scarcity and urgency are powerful motivators. We'll delve into strategies for creating a sense of limited availability and the fear of missing out (FOMO) to drive action. Additionally, we'll explore how exclusivity can add allure to your offers.

Examples of Irresistible Offers

While theory provides a solid foundation, real-world examples offer invaluable insights. We'll delve into a few examples of some of the most successful irresistible offers to date, showcasing how these businesses artfully applied psychological principles and crafting strategies discussed in this chapter to create offers that captured the hearts and wallets of their target audiences.

1. The Dollar Shave Club: A Razor Revolution

The Dollar Shave Club, a disruptor in the razor industry, completely redefined the way men approached shaving. Their subscription service delivered high-quality razors directly to customers' doors at a fraction of the cost of traditional brands. This is how Dollar Shave Club's irresistible offer addressed the common consumer pain point of overpriced razors with a humorous and straightforward approach.

Offer Overview

Dollar Shave Club's offer, represented by their subscription model, was revolutionary in its simplicity. They communicated the value of their offer effectively, emphasizing not just the quality of their razors but also the convenience and affordability. This subscription model not only transformed the way customers bought razors but also cultivated a loyal customer base.

Application of Psychology and Crafting Principles

Dollar Shave Club employed psychology to create a compelling offer. They leveraged the psychological factors of humor, convenience, and cost-savings. The witty marketing campaigns and straightforward messaging resonated with consumers, breaking down barriers and objections.

Results and Impact

The Dollar Shave Club's offer had a seismic impact on the industry. They disrupted established razor brands and garnered a massive customer following. By addressing the pain points head-on and delivering exceptional value, they achieved remarkable success. The subscription-based model not only drove significant revenue but also created brand loyalty among subscribers.

Key Takeaways:

- Simplicity and clarity in messaging can be exceptionally persuasive.

- Humor can disarm objections and make an offer memorable.

- Addressing common consumer pain points directly can create a strong emotional connection.

- Subscription models can foster customer loyalty and recurring revenue.

2. Airbnb: Creating a Sense of Belonging

Airbnb revolutionized the travel industry by tapping into the desire for unique experiences and authentic connections. This is how Airbnb's irresistible offer of "belonging anywhere" resonated with travelers' aspirations for authenticity and connection.

Offer Overview

Airbnb's offer went beyond providing accommodation; it offered the promise of immersive travel experiences. Their platform allowed hosts to share their spaces and travelers to immerse themselves in local culture. This is how their offer catered to the emotional needs of both hosts and guests.

Application of Psychology and Crafting Principles

Airbnb skillfully employed psychological triggers such as trust, authenticity, and community. By vetting hosts and guests, they built trust and credibility. Their platform facilitated emotional connections by enabling travelers to fulfill their aspirations of exploring new places while providing hosts with income opportunities.

Results and Impact

Airbnb's irresistible offer transformed the travel industry. They created a global community of hosts and travelers, facilitating authentic cultural exchanges. Their impact extended beyond travel, influencing the hospitality sector and redefining the concept of 'home away from home.' Airbnb's offer resulted in significant revenue generation and market dominance.

Key Takeaways:

- Trust and credibility are paramount, especially in peer-to-peer platforms.

- Appeals to authentic experiences and connections can resonate deeply.

- Building a sense of community around your offer can foster brand loyalty.

3. MasterClass: Learning from the Masters

MasterClass revolutionized online education by offering access to world-class expertise with celebrity instructors. MasterClass crafted an irresistible offer that tapped into the customer's desire for self-improvement and mastery.

Offer Overview

MasterClass's offer was simple yet profoundly compelling: learn from the best in the world. By featuring renowned instructors across diverse fields, they provided unparalleled value and exclusivity. MasterClass connected learners with their instructors, creating a sense of personal mentorship.

Application of Psychology and Crafting Principles

MasterClass used psychological elements such as authority, expertise, and personalization to make their offer irresistible. They leveraged the reputations of celebrity instructors to establish credibility and create a strong emotional connection between learners and mentors.

Results and Impact:

MasterClass's offer disrupted the online education landscape. They brought unparalleled expertise to learners worldwide, democratizing access to world-class instruction. MasterClass achieved considerable market share, impressive revenue figures, and an enduring place in the e-learning industry.

Key Takeaways:

- Associating your offer with authorities and experts can boost credibility.

- Personalized learning experiences can create strong emotional connections.

- Offering exclusive access to knowledge can be highly persuasive.

These examples showcase how these businesses strategically applied psychological principles and crafting strategies to create irresistible offers. By analyzing their success stories, you can glean valuable insights to apply to your own offer creation endeavors.

Chapter Two

HormoziGPT

A s we mentioned earlier ChatGPT works by understanding the context of your questions and prompts, allowing it to provide coherent and contextually relevant responses. Whether you need research assistance, content creation, or brainstorming ideas, ChatGPT is here to assist you. It's like having an AI-powered brainstorming partner at your side 24/7.

Exploring the Qualities of Alex Hormozi

Now, let's shift our focus to the entrepreneurial brilliance of Alex Hormozi. If you're unfamiliar with Alex, you're in for a treat. He's a renowned figure in the world of business and entrepreneurship, known for his extraordinary ability to craft irresistible offers that drive massive success.

Alex Hormozi's key strengths include:

1. Strategic Vision: Alex has an uncanny ability to see opportunities where others see obstacles. He's a visionary thinker who can spot market gaps and devise innovative solutions.

2. Bold Execution: One of Alex's defining traits is his willingness to take bold actions. He doesn't just come up with ideas; he executes them with conviction and determination.

3. Relentless Learning: Alex's success is a result of his relentless pursuit of knowledge. He's always learning, staying ahead of the curve, and adapting to changing market dynamics.

4. Mastery of Offers: Above all, Alex Hormozi is a master at crafting irresistible offers. He understands the psychology of customers, knows how to connect with their emotions, and delivers value that exceeds expectations.

Benefits of Using ChatGPT for Creating Offers

Now, here's where the magic begins. Combining ChatGPT's capabilities with the entrepreneurial prowess of Alex Hormozi can be a game-changer for your business. Here are some key benefits of using ChatGPT in your offer creation process:

1. Knowledge Amplification: ChatGPT serves as your knowledge amplifier, providing instant access to vast information. You can use it to research market trends, gather competitive intelligence, and stay informed about your industry.

2. Idea Generation: Stuck in a creative rut? ChatGPT can help spark innovative ideas for your offers. It's a brainstorming partner that never tires and can offer fresh perspectives on your business.

3. Copywriting Assistance: Crafting persuasive copy is an art, and Alex Hormozi is a master at it. With ChatGPT, you can enhance your copywriting skills by generating compelling headlines, persuasive sales pitches, and attention-grabbing hooks.

4. Offer Refinement: Alex Hormozi's offer crafting strategies are renowned for their effectiveness. ChatGPT can assist you in fine-tuning your offers to align with his principles and maximize their irresistibility.

Chapter Three

Offer Ideation

We're about to embark on a journey that will demystify the art of crafting irresistible offers. Offers so compelling that your customers won't just say "yes"; they'll practically jump at the opportunity. It's a bit like turning water into wine but in the world of business. So, grab a comfy seat and let's dive into the secrets of crafting offers that command attention and action.

The Power of an Irresistible Offer

Before we plunge into the nitty-gritty of irresistible offers, let's ponder the question: Why bother creating a great offer in the first place? Well, it's quite simple.

Imagine you're in the market for a landing page for your pesto business. You've got two options on the table:

Option A: "I will create a landing page for you for $500."

Option B: "I'll design a customized landing page for you, interview 10 of your target customers to understand their innermost desires, and then use that information to write world-class copy for your landing page. You don't pay me until your page reaches $10,000 in sales. And did I mention my 'no pesto, no paper' guarantee? You won't pay unless you're 100% satisfied with your results. The cost is $2,000."

Now, take a moment to think. Both options promise the same thing—a landing page. But if you're anything like the savvy consumer we know you are, you'd choose Option B faster than a seagull swooping in on a beach picnic. Why? Because Option B is a textbook example of an irresistible offer.

In the early days, I, too, believed that an offer was merely the product or service you were selling. Whether it was copywriting, landing page creation, or even cat meme creation (hey, don't underestimate the power of cute cats), I thought it was all about what you sold. But, as I waded deeper into the realms of marketing wizardry, I uncovered a profound truth.

Your offer isn't just what you sell; it's how you package and frame the value you provide to your customers. It's about presenting it in a way that makes it almost impossible for them to say "no." In essence, it's like wrapping a gift in the shiniest, most enticing paper you can find.

The Value Equation

Now that you're on board with the importance of crafting irresistible offers, let me introduce you to a simple yet potent framework that aligns perfectly with the teachings of Alex Hormozi. Think of it as the secret sauce to your offer creation endeavors.

We'll call it the "Value Equation," and it's as straightforward as a classic Margherita pizza. Simplicity at its finest, but oh so effective.

Alex Hormozi's Value Equation

Hormozi's genius lies in his ability to break down the value of an offer into four key parameters:

1. The Dream Outcome: This is the creme de la creme—the ultimate prize. What's the absolute best possible outcome your product or service can deliver to your customers? We're talking dreams coming true here.

2. The Likelihood of Achievement: Now, let's get practical. How likely is it that your customers will actually reach that dream outcome once they've taken the plunge and purchased your offer?

3. The Time Delay: Patience may be a virtue, but in the world of irresistible offers, time matters. How long does it take for your customers to achieve that dream outcome after they've made the purchase?

4. The Effort & Sacrifice: Last but not least, we have the effort and sacrifice factor. How much blood, sweat, and tears (figuratively, we hope) do your customers need to invest to reach that dream outcome?

Let's distill this into one golden sentence: To create irresistible offers, you need to maximize the Dream Outcome and Likelihood of Achievement while minimizing the Time Delay and Effort and Sacrifice required.

Sounds great, doesn't it? But I get it; mapping out this equation for your own offer can feel a bit like deciphering ancient hieroglyphics. Fear not, my friend, for I have a solution that'll make this process as smooth as a silk tie on a Sunday morning.

The Hormozi-fier Prompt

Cue the drumroll! The Hormozi-fier Prompt is your ticket to crafting irresistible offers faster than you can say "value bomb."

Step 1: Rank Your Offer

In the first step of the prompt, you'll receive:

- Scores for each of the four value equation components.

- An overall "Offer Score" that rates your offer's irresistibility.

- Actionable suggestions on how to enhance each component of the value equation.

- Two suggestions for alternative offers that could potentially have even higher offer scores.

Now, let's get to the heart of it. Here's the first prompt:

[Act as Alex Hormozi and rate my offer. For context, my offer is to:**[DESCRIBE YOUR OFFER]**

---You should rate my offer based on Alex Hormozi's 4-part value equation framework:

1) How desirable is this offer's dream outcome from a scale of 1-100? ("Dream Score")

2) How high is the offer's perceived likelihood of achievement on a scale of 1-100? ("Success Score")

3) How high is the offer's perceived time delay between purchasing the product and reaching the promised achievement on a scale from 0 to 1? ("Time Score") The higher the time delay, the higher the score. Ideally, the perceived time delay should be as low as possible.

4) How high is the offer's perceived effort and sacrifice on a scale of 0 to 1? ("Effort Score") The higher the perceived effort, the higher the score. Ideally, the perceived effort and sacrifice should be as low as possible.

After rating each of the 4 components, calculate an "offer score", which is calculated like this:

1) Multiply "Dream Score" with "Success Score"

2) Multiply "Time score" with "Effort Score"

3) Divide the product of the Dream & Success score with the product of the Time and Effort Score to get the "offer score"

In your output, provide actionable advice for how I can tweak my offer to get a higher score on each of the 4 components of the value equation framework.

Also advise me on 2 other offer structures with higher offer score that I could consider instead of my current one, and explain why they have a higher score.]

In this step, you rate your offer based on Alex Hormozi's four-part value equation framework:

Dream Score: How desirable is your offer's dream outcome on a scale of 1-100?

Success Score: How likely is it that your customers will achieve the dream outcome on a scale of 1-100?

Time Score: What's the perceived time delay between purchasing your product and reaching the promised achievement, on a scale from 0 to 1?

Effort Score: How high is the perceived effort and sacrifice required on a scale of 0 to 1?

The magic happens when you calculate your "offer score" using these components. Here's how:

Multiply "Dream Score" by "Success Score."

Multiply "Time Score" by "Effort Score."

Divide the product of the Dream and Success scores by the product of the Time and Effort scores to get your "offer score."

In your output, you'll receive valuable advice on how to enhance each of these four components to make your offer truly irresistible.

But here's where it gets even more exciting.

Step 2: Let Hormozi Create an Irresistible Offer for You

After completing Step 1, you can take things up a notch. Use this prompt to let Alex Hormozi himself improve your offer until it reaches a perfect offer score of 1,000,000, aligning with the best possible values:

It's like having a master offer creator fine-tune your offer to perfection.

PROMPT 2 [Tweak this offer as much as you want so that it reaches a perfect offer score of 1,000,000

(Dream Score = 100, Success Score = 100, Time Score = 0.1, Effort Score = 0.1)]

Here's an example of me using the prompt in regard to this eBook

Step 1 Response:

[Offer Description: Your offer is a $0.99 ebook that spans fewer than 30 pages, providing concise instructions for Alex Hormozi fans on how to transform ChatGPT into a tool for crafting irresistible offers for their businesses. Additionally, you'll offer an audiobook version of the book and a $99 video course demonstrating various ways to leverage AI and ChatGPT for business purposes.

Now, let's assess this offer using Alex Hormozi's four-part value equation framework:

1) Dream Score (Desirability): On a scale of 1-100, the dream outcome for this offer is highly desirable. ChatGPT fans seeking to emulate Alex Hormozi's success would find immense value in learning how to turn ChatGPT into a powerful tool for crafting irresistible offers. I'd rate the Dream Score as 95.

2) Success Score (Likelihood of Achievement): Given the practical nature of the instructions and the clear value proposition, the likelihood of customers achieving their desired outcome (emulating Alex Hormozi's style) is relatively high. I'd rate the Success Score as 90.

3) Time Score (Time Delay): The perceived time delay between purchasing the ebook and achieving the desired outcome is minimal. Readers can start implementing the strategies immediately. I'd rate the Time Score as 0.05.

4) Effort Score (Effort and Sacrifice): The perceived effort and sacrifice required by customers to benefit from this offer are quite low. The ebook offers straightforward instructions, and the audiobook version provides flexibility. I'd rate the Effort Score as 0.1.

Now, let's calculate the "offer score" using these scores:

- Dream Score (95) x Success Score (90) = 8,550

- Time Score (0.05) x Effort Score (0.1) = 0.005

- Offer Score = (8,550) / (0.005) = 1,710,000

The calculated offer score is an impressive 1,710,000. This suggests that your offer is already quite strong, aligning well with Alex Hormozi's principles.

Actionable Advice: Given the high offer score, there's minimal need for improvement. However, consider enhancing the marketing and positioning of the offer to reach a broader audience of ChatGPT enthusiasts looking to excel in business.

Alternative Offer Structures: While your current offer performs exceptionally well, here are two alternative structures with even higher offer scores:

Alternative Offer 1: Personalized ChatGPT Offer Optimization Service

Offer Description: For a fee of $499, you provide a personalized offer optimization service. You'll work directly with clients, leveraging ChatGPT's capabilities to craft irresistible offers tailored to their specific businesses.

Dream Score: 97 (Customized offer optimization)

Success Score: 92 (Hands-on guidance)

Time Score: 0.04 (Prompt results)

Effort Score: 0.08 (Moderate client involvement) Offer Score: 233,500

Alternative Offer 2: ChatGPT Masterclass Series

Offer Description: Offer a comprehensive ChatGPT Masterclass Series, priced at $199. This series includes in-depth training on various applications of ChatGPT for business, including crafting irresistible offers, content generation, and customer engagement.

- Dream Score: 94 (Comprehensive training) Success Score: 88 (Extensive knowledge transfer)

- Time Score: 0.08 (Multiple modules delivered over time)

- Effort Score: 0.06 (Moderate learning curve)

- Offer Score: 88,500

Both alternative offers score well, with unique advantages depending on your target audience and objectives.

Remember, your initial offer is already strong, but these alternatives provide different avenues to consider for maximizing your offer's appeal and value.]

Step 2 Response:

[To achieve a perfect offer score of 1,000,000 based on the value equation framework, we need to make significant adjustments to your offer. Here's an enhanced offer that aligns with these criteria:

Offer: "AI Mastery Unleashed - Total Business Transformation"

Ebook:

A comprehensive ebook (200+ pages) offering a deep dive into leveraging ChatGPT for business transformation.

Includes real-world case studies, actionable strategies, and expert insights.

Price: $19.99

Audiobook:

A professionally narrated audiobook version of the ebook for auditory learners and busy entrepreneurs.

Price: Included with the ebook purchase.

Video Course:

A comprehensive video course consisting of 10 modules with over 50 hours of content.

Covers advanced AI techniques, practical implementation, and personalized coaching.

Includes access to a private mastermind community for ongoing support and networking.

Price: $499

Additional Bonuses:

One-on-One Strategy Session: A 60-minute personalized strategy session with an AI and ChatGPT expert to kickstart your transformation. (Value: $299)

AI Tools and Resources: Access to a library of AI tools, templates, and resources to streamline implementation. (Value: $199)

Lifetime Updates: Free lifetime updates to the ebook, audiobook, and video course to keep you at the forefront of AI technology. (Value: Priceless)

Total Offer Price: $699 (One-time payment)

Now, let's calculate the offer score for this enhanced offer:

Dream Score: 100

Success Score: 100

Time Score: 0.1

Effort Score: 0.1

Offer Score = (Dream Score * Success Score) / (Time Score * Effort Score)

Offer Score = (100 * 100) / (0.1 * 0.1) = 1,000,000

With this revised offer, you achieve a perfect offer score of 1,000,000. Here's why it achieves a high score:

Dream Score (100): The offer promises comprehensive knowledge and success, covering all aspects of ChatGPT's impact on business.

Success Score (100): The offer includes extensive content, one-on-one support, and a community for success assurance.

Time Score (0.1): The offer provides quick access to resources and support, minimizing time delays.

Effort Score (0.1): The offer includes templates, resources, and a strategy session to reduce perceived effort.

This enhanced offer provides exceptional value, making it highly desirable and achievable for your target audience, while minimizing time and effort constraints.]

If you'd like to download the Prompts in PDF Form for easier access please visit **https://docdro.id/vwP6WmK**

Chapter Four

Crafting
Irresistible Offers

W elcome to the heart of irresistible offer creation. In this chapter, you'll learn the art and science of crafting offers that your audience simply can't resist. Irresistible offers are the lifeblood of any successful business, and mastering this skill will set you apart from the competition.

Identifying Your Unique Selling Points (USPs) and Creating a Unique Value Proposition (UVP)

Before we delve into the intricacies of crafting irresistible offers, it's essential to lay the foundation by identifying your Unique Selling Points (USPs) and creating a Unique Value Proposition (UVP). These elements serve as the building blocks of an offer that stands out and captures your audience's attention.

Understanding USPs

Your Unique Selling Points (USPs) are the distinct advantages or features that differentiate your product or service from competitors. Think of them as the special ingredients that make your bakery's pastries unique. Collaborate with ChatGPT to brainstorm and identify the key aspects that set your offer apart.

Creating Your Unique Value Proposition (UVP):

Once you've pinpointed your USPs, it's time to craft a Unique Value Proposition (UVP) that communicates the specific benefits your offer provides to your target audience. This is akin to creating a recipe that showcases the exceptional qualities of your pastries. Work with ChatGPT to articulate a UVP that resonates with your audience.

Action: Identify Your Unique Selling Points (USPs): Collaborate with ChatGPT to identify the unique features, benefits, or qualities of your product or service that set it apart from competitors.

Prompt for ChatGPT: "List the unique selling points (USPs) of [describe your product or service]. What makes it stand out in the market? Provide details on its distinctive features, benefits, or qualities."

Craft Your Unique Value Proposition (UVP)

Work with ChatGPT to create a compelling Unique Value Proposition (UVP) based on the identified USPs. Use the following prompt as a starting point:

Prompt for ChatGPT: "Craft a Unique Value Proposition (UVP) for [describe your product or service]. Highlight the specific benefits and advantages it offers to your target audience. Make sure it communicates the unique qualities that make your offer irresistible."

Writing Compelling Headlines and Hooks

The Power of the First Impression

Your headline is the first thing your audience sees, and it's your one chance to make a memorable impression. Whether it's a sales page, email subject line, or social media post, your headlines and hooks play a crucial role in capturing attention.

The Psychology of Headlines

Understanding the psychology behind headlines is the first step. What makes a headline compelling? Why do some headlines grab your attention while others go unnoticed? We'll dive into the secrets of writing headlines that stop the scroll.

Great headlines often tap into the desires, fears, or curiosity of your target audience. They should create a sense of urgency or promise a solution to a burning problem. For example, a headline like "Unlock the Secret to Doubling Your Income in 30 Days" not only piques curiosity but also offers a clear benefit.

Action: Collaborate with ChatGPT to analyze successful headlines across various industries. Break down the elements that make them effective, such as curiosity, urgency, and relevance. Instruct ChatGPT to brainstorm headline ideas tailored to your specific offers using the following prompt:

Prompt for ChatGPT: "Generate compelling headlines for **[describe your offer]**. Focus on creating a sense of **[choose an emotion or benefit relevant to your offer, e.g., urgency, excitement, curiosity]**. Ensure the headlines are concise and attention-grabbing."

Crafting Magnetic Hooks

Hooks are the intriguing phrases or questions that keep your audience reading. They're the bridge between your headline and the rest of your offer. We'll explore techniques for crafting hooks that pull readers deeper into your content.

Hooks should draw readers in and make them hungry for more. They can be personal anecdotes, thought-provoking questions, or bold statements. For example, a hook like "Imagine a life where you work less, earn more, and live on your terms" sets a compelling tone for an offer related to work-life balance or entrepreneurship.

Action: Instruct ChatGPT on the elements of creating hooks that align with your offer's value proposition. Show it how to use storytelling, questions, or surprising facts to engage the audience. Encourage ChatGPT to generate hooks for your specific offers with the following prompt:

Prompt for ChatGPT: "Craft engaging hooks for **[describe your offer]**. These hooks should captivate the reader and encourage them to explore further. Use storytelling, questions, or intriguing statements to achieve this."

Structuring Your Offer for Maximum Impact

The Art of Persuasive Presentation

It's not just what you say; it's how you say it. The structure of your offer can significantly impact its effectiveness. Whether it's a sales letter, video script, or webinar, we'll dissect the anatomy of a high-converting offer.

The Power of Flow

A well-structured offer takes your audience on a journey. It guides them from problem recognition to solution acceptance. We'll break down the essential components of offer structure, from the introduction to the call to action.

The flow of your offer should mirror the natural progression of your prospect's thoughts. It should start by addressing a problem they relate to, present your solution as the answer, and provide evidence to support your claims. Finally, it should guide them to take action, whether it's making a purchase or subscribing to your newsletter.

Action: Collaborate with ChatGPT to outline the ideal structure for your specific offers. Teach ChatGPT how to create a roadmap that leads the audience through the offer seamlessly using the following prompt:

Prompt for ChatGPT: "Map out the structure of **[describe your offer]**. Begin with a compelling introduction that addresses the reader's pain points. Then, guide them through the solution and provide evidence of its effectiveness. Finally, craft a persuasive call to action. Ensure the flow is natural and engaging."

Crafting Compelling Stories

Stories are the emotional glue that binds your offer to your audience. We'll explore the art of storytelling and how to weave narratives that resonate with your prospects.

Stories should transport your audience into a relatable scenario where they can envision themselves benefiting from your offer. They can be success stories of previous customers, personal anecdotes, or hypothetical situations that showcase the transformation your product or service can bring. Stories add depth and authenticity to your offer.

Action: Instruct ChatGPT on the elements of effective storytelling, such as relatable characters, relatable problems, and triumphant resolutions. Collaborate with ChatGPT to generate story ideas that enhance your offer's emotional appeal using the following prompt:

Prompt for ChatGPT: "Craft compelling stories that align with **[describe your offer]**. These stories should resonate with the audience and illustrate the positive impact of your offer. Use relatable characters and situations to make the stories engaging."

Incorporating Scarcity and Urgency

The Motivating Forces

Scarcity and urgency are powerful psychological triggers that prompt action. We'll uncover how to incorporate these elements into your offers without resorting to manipulative tactics.

Scarcity: Less Is More

Scarcity involves limiting the availability of your offer. It creates a sense of exclusivity and compels your audience to act quickly. We'll discuss ethical scarcity tactics that drive conversions.

Scarcity tactics can include limited-time offers, limited quantities, or exclusive access for a select group. For example, "Only 50 spots available for our exclusive coaching program" leverages scarcity to encourage quick decisions.

Action: Teach ChatGPT the principles of ethical scarcity and how to implement them in your offers. Collaborate to create scarcity-driven strategies tailored to your specific offers using the following prompt:

Prompt for ChatGPT: "Incorporate ethical scarcity into **[describe your offer]**. Brainstorm strategies like limited-time offers, exclusive access, or limited quantities that create a sense of urgency without being manipulative."

Urgency: Now Is the Time

Urgency is about conveying the importance of taking action immediately. It's the motivator that prevents procrastination. We'll explore how to communicate urgency effectively.

Urgency can be communicated through compelling language, countdown timers, or time-sensitive bonuses. An offer like "Enroll now to secure your spot and receive a bonus worth $500, but act fast, this offer ends tonight" utilizes urgency to drive immediate action.

Action: Collaborate with ChatGPT to craft urgency-driven messaging for your offers. Show ChatGPT how to use persuasive language and visual cues to convey the importance of immediate action using the following prompt:

Prompt for ChatGPT: "Create urgency-driven messages for **[describe your offer]**. Use persuasive language to emphasize the need for immediate action."

Now that you've learned the principles of creating compelling offers, you might be wondering how your current offers measure up. For a limited time, I'm offering readers of this book an exclusive **Personalized Offer Audit** Service. For just $97, I'll review your offer and provide detailed, actionable feedback to help you maximize its effectiveness. The audit takes a few days to complete so there are limited spots available. Secure your spot before they're gone. **Scan the QR code** below to learn more and take your offers to the next level.

Chapter Five

Testing Your Offers for Irresistibility

The Crucial Role of Testing

Imagine you're an artisan baker, and you've just created a new pastry recipe. You're confident it's delicious, but before you unveil it to the world, you decide to host a tasting event with a select group of pastry enthusiasts. Their feedback is invaluable because it helps you tweak the recipe, ensuring it's nothing short of perfection when it reaches your bakery's display case.

Testing your offers is akin to this pastry tasting event. It's your chance to gather feedback, fine-tune your offer, and make sure it resonates with your target audience. In this chapter, we'll explore the art and science of A/B testing, data analysis, and iterative refinement.

A/B Testing Your Offers

A/B testing, also known as split testing, is a method that allows you to compare two versions of an offer to determine which one performs better. The goal is to identify the elements that resonate most with your audience and improve your offer's conversion rates.

Collaborating with ChatGPT for A/B Testing
Action:

Identifying Testing Variables:

• Collaborate with ChatGPT to identify the variables you want to test in your offers. For instance, if you're selling a subscription service, you might want to test different pricing tiers, copy variations, or even the color of your call-to-action buttons. Use a prompt like, "Help me identify key variables for A/B testing in our subscription service offer."

Creating A/B Test Variations:

Instruct ChatGPT to generate content variations for your A/B tests. For example, if you're testing email subject lines, you could prompt, "Generate five different email subject lines for our A/B test, each with a unique approach."

Analyzing A/B Test Results:

Leverage ChatGPT's analytical abilities to interpret A/B test results. Provide ChatGPT with your Data and a prompt such as, "Review the A/B test data and provide insights into which variation performed better, and why."

Iterative Testing Strategy:

Collaborate with ChatGPT to outline a strategy for ongoing A/B testing and optimization. Use a prompt like, "Help me create a plan for continuous A/B testing and optimization to ensure our offers remain competitive."

Analyzing Data and Making Data-Driven Decisions

In today's digital age, data is more than just numbers; it's a treasure trove of insights waiting to be discovered. Analyzing data is a crucial step in understanding your audience, their behavior, and how they interact with your offers.

Leveraging ChatGPT for Data Analysis

Action:

Data Interpretation:

Collaborate with ChatGPT to interpret data and extract actionable insights. Use a prompt like, "Analyze this data to identify patterns and trends in customer behavior, and provide recommendations based on your findings."

Predictive Analysis:

Explore predictive analysis with ChatGPT to forecast future trends and customer preferences. Prompt ChatGPT with, "Use historical data to predict potential shifts in customer preferences and suggest preemptive strategies."

Competitor Analysis:

Instruct ChatGPT to conduct competitive analysis based on available data. For instance, "Analyze competitor data to identify gaps and opportunities in our market positioning and offers."

Iterating and Improving Your Offers Based on Feedback

Your offers are not set in stone; they're dynamic and should evolve based on feedback and changing market conditions. Continuous improvement is the key to keeping your offers irresistibly fresh and relevant.

ChatGPT-Powered Feedback Loop

Action:

Feedback Collection:

Collaborate with ChatGPT to develop a system for collecting feedback from customers. For example, "Create a feedback survey to gather input from recent offer purchasers, focusing on their experiences and suggestions for improvement."

Feedback Analysis:

Leverage ChatGPT to analyze feedback data and extract actionable insights. Use a prompt like, "Analyze customer feedback to identify common pain points and areas where our offers can be enhanced."

Iterative Refinement:

Instruct ChatGPT to propose iterative changes and refinements to your offers based on feedback analysis. For instance, "Based on customer feedback, suggest specific improvements to our pricing structure and messaging to address common concerns."

Content Optimization:

Collaborate with ChatGPT to optimize offer content and messaging based on feedback. Prompt ChatGPT with, "Generate revised offer descriptions and promotional materials incorporating customer-suggested improvements."

The Continuous Cycle of Testing and Optimization

Testing, data analysis, and iterative improvement should become a recurring cycle in your offer crafting process. Your goal is not just to create irresistible offers but to ensure they stay that way in a dynamic market.

Testing and optimizing your offers is the bridge that transforms good ideas into irresistible offers. With the power of A/B testing, data analysis, and continuous refinement, you can fine-tune your offers to resonate deeply with your audience, driving higher conversion rates and customer satisfaction.

In the next chapter, we'll explore advanced strategies for scaling your irresistible offers to a massive audience. Get ready to take your offers to the big leagues and unlock their full potential.

Chapter Six

Scaling Your Offers to a Massive Audience

W elcome to the exciting world of scaling your irresistible offers with the help of ChatGPT. In this chapter, we will explore comprehensive strategies and tactics to extend your reach, engage a vast audience, and unlock the infinite potential of your offers.

The Power of Scaling

From Thousands to Millions

Scaling isn't just about growing your business; it's about expanding your impact. It's the transition from serving a limited customer base to reaching millions of potential clients. However, successful scaling requires a well-crafted plan, and collaboration with ChatGPT can be your secret weapon.

Define Your Scaling Goals:

Start by specifying your scaling objectives. What audience size are you targeting, and over what timeframe? Be clear about your goals before involving ChatGPT.

ChatGPT's Data Analysis:

Prompt ChatGPT to analyze market data and identify potential markets and demographics ripe for expansion. For example, "Please analyze market data and identify potential markets and demographics that show growth potential for our scaling strategy."

Content Generation:

Instruct ChatGPT to generate engaging content ideas for your chosen digital channels. For instance, "Generate a series of blog post ideas that resonate with our target audience and align with our scaling goals."

Customer Segmentation:

Collaborate with ChatGPT to segment your audience effectively. Provide a prompt like, "Help me create customer segments based on demographics, preferences, and behavior to tailor our offers and messaging."

Leveraging Digital Channels

In today's digital age, scaling has never been more accessible. The internet offers a multitude of channels and platforms to promote your irresistible offers. From social media to email marketing, we'll explore how to leverage these digital avenues.

Strategies for Scaling

Automation: Your Secret Weapon

Automation is the catalyst for scaling. It allows you to maintain efficiency and consistency while reaching a larger audience. Whether it's automating your marketing, sales, or customer support, lets dive into the world of automation.

ChatGPT for Automation

Action: Work with ChatGPT to identify areas in a business where automation can be applied for scaling. Teach it how to choose the right automation tools and platforms.

Content Automation:

Prompt ChatGPT to automate content generation. For example, "Automate the creation of social media posts and blog content that aligns with our scaling strategy."

Chatbots for Support:

ChatGPT can set up chatbots for customer support.

Email Campaigns:

Collaborate with ChatGPT to automate email marketing campaigns. Provide a prompt such as, "How can we automate our email marketing campaigns, including personalized content and audience segmentation?"

Building Strategic Partnerships

Collaboration doesn't end with ChatGPT. Building strategic partnerships can be a game-changer. We'll explore how collaboration with other businesses, influencers, or industry leaders can open new avenues for growth.

Collaboration Strategies with ChatGPT

Action: Work alongside ChatGPT to identify potential collaboration opportunities:

Partnership Research:

Prompt ChatGPT to research potential partners or businesses in your niche. For example, "Research businesses and influencers in our industry who align with our brand and could be potential partners."

Collaborative Content:

Collaborate with ChatGPT to brainstorm ideas for collaborative content. Provide a prompt like, "Generate ideas for collaborative content with potential partners."

Influencer Identification:

Leverage ChatGPT to identify suitable influencers in your industry. Use a prompt such as, "Identify influencers with a significant following in our niche and analyze their engagement metrics."

Challenges and Pitfalls

The Art of Scaling Without Losing Quality

One challenge in scaling is maintaining the quality of your offers as you reach a larger audience. We'll delve into strategies for upholding the standards that make your offers irresistible.

Quality Assurance with ChatGPT

Action: Collaborate with ChatGPT to implement quality assurance measures:

Quality Control Processes:

Instruct ChatGPT to assist in developing and implementing quality control processes. For example, "Help create processes that ensure consistent product or service quality during rapid growth."

Training and Guidelines:

Collaborate with ChatGPT to create training materials and guidelines for your team. Use a prompt like, "Create training materials that emphasize the importance of maintaining quality standards."

Avoiding Overextension

Scaling too quickly can lead to overextension. We'll discuss the risks associated with aggressive scaling and how to navigate them.

Strategic Scaling Decisions with ChatGPT

Action: Collaborate with ChatGPT to make strategic scaling decisions:

Scalability Assessment:

Use ChatGPT to assess your business's readiness for scaling. Consider factors like financial stability, operational capacity, and market demand before expanding aggressively. For example, "Evaluate our readiness for scaling by analyzing financial stability and operational capacity."

Risk Analysis:

Instruct ChatGPT to perform risk analysis related to scaling decisions. Prompt it with, "Analyze potential risks associated with rapid scaling and provide insights on risk mitigation."

The Infinite Potential

Scaling your offers to a massive audience is where the magic happens. It's the path to crafting $100 million offers that change industries and leave a lasting legacy. Get ready to unlock the secrets of increasing conversions and driving unprecedented success in Chapter 7.

Chapter Seven

Maximizing Conversion Rates

U nderstanding and optimizing conversion rates is a critical aspect of crafting irresistible offers. After all, the ultimate goal is to not just attract potential customers but also to convert them into loyal clients. In this chapter, we'll explore the factors that influence conversion rates, strategies to optimize your offers for higher conversions, and the implementation of persuasive techniques to seal the deal.

Understanding the Factors that Influence Conversion Rates

Before we delve into the art of optimization, let's take a moment to understand what drives conversion rates. Conversion rate is the percentage of visitors to your offer who take a desired action, such as making a purchase or signing up for a newsletter. Several key factors influence these rates:

1. Offer Relevance: Your offer must align with the needs, desires, and pain points of your target audience. It's like serving a refreshing lemonade on a scorching summer day – exactly what people are craving.

2. User Experience: The ease of navigating your offer, the clarity of your messaging, and the simplicity of the conversion process all impact conversion rates. Think of it as providing clear signposts and a smooth path to your bakery's front door.

3. Trust and Credibility: As discussed in the previous chapter, trust plays a significant role. Visitors are more likely to convert if they trust your brand and believe in the value of your offer.

4. Incentives: Sometimes, a little nudge in the form of discounts, bonuses, or limited-time offers can significantly boost conversion rates. It's akin to offering a free pastry with every purchase – an irresistible incentive.

5. Social Proof (to be discussed in Chapter 8): When potential customers see others who have benefited from your offer, it creates a sense of trust and social validation. It's like having a bustling café with happy diners visible through the window.

Now that we have a grasp of what influences conversion rates let's move on to optimizing your offers.

Optimizing Your Offer for Higher Conversions

Optimizing your offer is like fine-tuning the recipe for your best-selling pastry. It's about making incremental improvements to achieve the perfect blend of taste and texture. Here's how you can optimize your offer for higher conversions:

1. **Conversion Funnel Optimization:** Your conversion funnel is a critical component of the customer journey. We'll discuss techniques to streamline and optimize each stage of the funnel.

Action: Collaborate with ChatGPT to map out your conversion funnel in intricate detail. Engage ChatGPT in analyzing user interactions at each stage of the funnel. Leverage its insights to identify potential bottlenecks and areas for improvement. Implement changes to streamline the process and reduce friction, guided by ChatGPT's data-driven recommendations. ChatGPT can help you craft persuasive messaging and create tailored content that addresses specific pain points or objections potential customers may have at each stage, ultimately increasing the likelihood of conversions.

2. Personalization: Tailoring your offers to individual customer preferences can skyrocket your conversion rates. Discover the power of personalized marketing.

Action: Empower ChatGPT to implement personalization strategies throughout the customer journey. Instruct ChatGPT to analyze user data and preferences, such as past interactions and purchase history. With this data, ChatGPT can assist in creating dynamic content that adapts to user behavior and preferences. Moreover, ChatGPT can help craft personalized recommendations and offers that resonate on a personal level with your audience. This level of personalization can substantially increase conversion rates by delivering precisely what each visitor is looking for.

3. Multivariate Testing: While we touched on A/B testing in Chapter 5, we'll now explore multivariate testing, a more advanced method for optimizing various elements of your offers simultaneously.

Action: Engage ChatGPT to set up multivariate tests for your offers. Work together to create variations that encompass various elements, such as headlines, images, pricing, and more. Collaborate with ChatGPT to design experiments that efficiently test these combinations. Analyze the results to gain a deep understanding of which elements work best in harmony to drive conversions. Implement changes based on these insights, and continually refine your offer to maximize its appeal and conversion potential.

Implementing Persuasive Techniques to Increase Conversion Rates

The art of persuasion is a powerful tool in your offer creation arsenal. Persuasion techniques can be the secret ingredient that convinces potential customers to take action. Here are some proven persuasive techniques:

1. Scarcity and Urgency: As we touched on earlier creating a sense of scarcity (limited availability) and urgency (limited time) can motivate quick decisions. It's like having a "Limited Edition" pastry that customers know won't be available for long.

2. Social Proof (to be discussed in Chapter 8): As mentioned earlier, social proof involves showcasing testimonials, reviews, and endorsements from satisfied customers. It's like having a wall of thank-you notes from delighted bakery patrons.

Action: Hold off on detailed social proof strategies until Chapter 8 when we dive into it more deeply.

3. Emotional Appeal: Appeals to emotions can be highly persuasive. Crafting stories or messaging that elicit specific emotions, such as joy, nostalgia, or empathy, can connect with your audience on a deeper level.

Action: Collaborate with ChatGPT to create emotionally resonant messaging that aligns with your brand and offer. Explore how different emotional triggers can influence your audience.

Understanding conversion rates, optimizing your offers, and employing persuasive techniques are essential steps in crafting irresistible offers. By making data-driven improvements, streamlining user experiences, and implementing ethical persuasion, you'll be well on your way to creating offers that not only attract but convert.

Chapter Eight

Building Trust
and Credibility

Welcome to the trust-building masterclass! In this chapter, we'll unravel the art of establishing trust and credibility with your audience. Trust is the cornerstone of any successful business relationship, and when it comes to crafting irresistible offers, it's non-negotiable. So, let's dive deep into the strategies and techniques that will make your offers not just enticing but also trusted and respected.

The Foundation of Trust

Imagine you're entering a quaint little bakery. The aroma of freshly baked bread fills the air, and the display case showcases an array of delectable pastries. But there's something unusual about this bakery—you can't see the bakers. You have no idea who's behind those mouthwatering creations. Would you feel comfortable buying a pastry, let alone investing in a whole cake for your special occasion?

Trust is the invisible baker in your business's kitchen. It's what makes customers feel at ease, confident, and willing to engage with your offers. Without trust, even the most irresistible offers might fall flat.

Why Trust Matters

Ease of Decision-Making: Trust reduces the perceived risk of making a purchase. It's like a comforting voice that says, "You're making the right choice."

Repeat Business: Customers who trust your brand are more likely to come back for more. It's like a friendly neighborhood café where everyone knows your name.

Word-of-Mouth: Satisfied and trusting customers become your brand advocates. They recommend your products or services to friends and family, like an enthusiastic foodie sharing a new restaurant discovery.

Now that we've established the significance of trust, let's explore how to build it effectively.

Establishing Trust with Your Audience

Trust isn't built overnight; it's nurtured through consistent actions, transparent communication, and genuine care for your audience. Here's how to lay the foundation:

1. Transparency

Openness is the first step in building trust. Be transparent about your offerings, pricing, and policies. It's like having a glass-walled kitchen in your bakery, so customers can see the baking process.

Action: Guide ChatGPT in creating clear and straightforward messaging about your offers. Ensure that product descriptions, pricing, and terms are easily accessible and easy to understand.

2. Authenticity

Authenticity breeds trust. Be genuine in your interactions with your audience. Share your brand's story, values, and mission. People connect with real stories, not marketing jargon.

Action: Collaborate with ChatGPT to craft an authentic brand story. Highlight your journey, challenges, and what sets your business apart.

3. Consistency

Consistency in your branding and messaging reinforces trust. It's like the familiar scent of your bakery's signature bread, assuring customers of the same quality every visit.

Action: Consult with ChatGPT to come up with a plan of maintaining a consistent brand voice and visual identity. Ensure that your website, social media, and marketing materials align with your brand's image.

4. Customer Support

Responsive and helpful customer support is a trust booster. Address inquiries, issues, and feedback promptly and professionally. It's like having attentive servers who cater to every customer's needs.

Action: Set up systems to provide excellent customer support. Teach ChatGPT Support Bots how to handle common customer queries and escalate issues when necessary.

Leveraging Social Proof and Testimonials

Social proof is a psychological phenomenon where people assume the actions of others in an attempt to reflect correct behavior for a given situation. In simpler terms, when others are doing it, we feel more confident doing it too. Here's how to use social proof effectively:

1. Customer Reviews

Encourage customers to leave reviews and ratings. Positive reviews act as endorsements for your offers. It's like having satisfied diners leave compliments on your restaurant's website.

Action: Collaborate with ChatGPT to develop strategies for gathering customer reviews. Set up automated review requests after purchases and showcase these reviews prominently.

2. Case Studies

Case studies offer in-depth insights into how your product or service has benefited customers. They provide tangible evidence of your value. It's like sharing success stories of couples who celebrated their anniversary at your restaurant.

Action: Work with ChatGPT to create engaging case studies that highlight specific customer experiences and outcomes. Use real data and testimonials to add credibility.

3. Influencer Endorsements

Partnering with influencers in your industry can provide powerful social proof. When respected figures vouch for your offers, it's like having renowned food critics give rave reviews.

Action: Identify potential influencers in your niche and explore collaboration opportunities. Teach ChatGPT how to identify influencers and create compelling partnership proposals for them.

Building Credibility Through Authority and Expertise

Establishing yourself as an authority in your field goes a long way in building credibility. When people perceive you as an expert, they're more likely to trust your offers. Here's how to position yourself as an authority:

1. Content Creation

Producing high-quality content that educates, informs, and entertains your audience is akin to hosting cooking classes to share your baking expertise. It's about crafting content that not only showcases your knowledge but also resonates with your audience's interests and needs.

Action: Collaborate with ChatGPT to generate valuable content that addresses your audience's pain points and questions. Work together on content ideas, outlines, and creation. Guide ChatGPT in researching relevant topics and crafting engaging blog posts, videos, or podcasts that provide real value to your audience.

ChatGPT Prompts:

- *"Brainstorm content ideas that align with our audience's interests and pain points."*

- *"Help me outline a blog post that addresses a common challenge our audience faces."*

- *"Let's create a video script that educates our viewers about a trending industry topic."*

2. Thought Leadership

Becoming a thought leader in your industry is like being the renowned chef who's interviewed by food magazines and invited to culinary conferences. It's about sharing your unique insights and opinions on industry trends and challenges, positioning yourself as an authority.

Action: Collaborate with ChatGPT on preparing and participating on platforms where you can share your insights with a wider audience. Additionally, guide ChatGPT on creating speeches or presentations for industry events where you can establish your thought leadership.

ChatGPT Prompts:

- *"Help me outline some Instagram Reel ideas that highlight our expertise in the industry."*

- *"Let's create a webinar presentation that shares our insights on the latest industry trends."*

- *"Assist me in drafting a thought-provoking speech for an upcoming industry conference."*

3. Certifications and Awards

Earning relevant certifications or industry awards can add a layer of credibility. It's like proudly displaying your bakery's "Best Pastry Shop of the Year" plaque.

Action: Collaborate with ChatGPT to identify certifications or industry awards that hold significance in your field. Instruct ChatGPT on the steps required to earn these accolades, including gathering necessary qualifications or documentation. Once achieved, integrate these certifications or awards into your marketing materials to showcase your expertise.

ChatGPT Prompts:

- *"Research industry certifications or awards that can enhance our credibility."*

- *"Outline the process to earn a specific industry certification."*

- *"Let's create a section in our marketing materials to prominently display our earned certifications and awards."*

Trust and credibility are the pillars upon which your irresistible offers stand. By being transparent, authentic, and consistent, you establish trust with your audience. Leveraging social proof and testimonials reinforces that trust. Finally, positioning yourself as an authority in your field builds long-lasting credibility.

Chapter Nine

Conclusion

C ongratulations on completing this journey into the world of irresistible offers! But remember, mastering the art of offer creation is an ongoing process. If you're serious about skyrocketing your conversion rates and harnessing the full potential of AI-powered copywriting, I highly recommend checking out **The AI-Powered Copywriting Playbook**. This in-depth guide will show you how to leverage cutting-edge technology to create copy that converts like crazy. As a valued reader of **100M Offers Made Easy**, you'll receive an exclusive discount. Don't wait – **Scan the QR Code** below to unlock your special offer and start crafting irresistible copy today!

Key Takeaways

Before we part ways, let's recap some of the key takeaways from our adventure:

The Power of an Irresistible Offer:

An irresistible offer isn't just about what you sell; it's about how you package and frame the value you provide to your customers.

Leveraging ChatGPT:

You've learned how to harness the incredible capabilities of ChatGPT to ideate, create, and refine your offers.

Testing and Optimization:

A/B testing, optimizing conversion funnels, and personalization are your allies in creating offers that continuously improve.

Building Trust and Credibility:

Trust is the cornerstone of any successful offer. Leveraging social proof, testimonials, and your expertise enhances your offer's credibility.

Maximizing Conversion Rates:

Understanding the factors that influence conversion rates and employing persuasive techniques are crucial for sealing the deal.

Your Feedback Matters

I hope this book has been an enlightening and practical resource on your journey to becoming a master offer creator. If you've enjoyed reading it and found value in its insights and strategies, I'd greatly appreciate it if you could take a moment to leave a review. Your feedback helps me improve and makes the book show up for more readers who can benefit from this knowledge.

Thank you for joining me on this quest to craft irresistible offers that not only transform businesses but also leave a lasting impact on customers. The power to create $100 million offers is within your grasp, and I'm excited to see the incredible offers you'll bring into the world.

Safe travels on your entrepreneurial adventures, and may your offers always be irresistible!